Meimei --- Let's Count!

měi měi   ràng wǒ men shǔ yì shǔ

美美 ----- 让 我 们 数 一 数!

written and illustrated by Yue Chen

Dedication

I dedicate this book to my beloved dad who has been so strong in fighting for his health and to my loving mom who is always present for her family, especially for her husband. They are 'UNITED AS ONE' through thick and thin, and all the ups and downs.

献给：我亲爱的爸爸和妈妈

HOW TO USE THIS BOOK

READING IN ENGLISH AND CHINESE:
You can read the book in English and substitute the numerical words with Chinese Pinyin. Match the highlighted English and Chinese scripts, and point to the corresponding numbers. For example: Yeah! We found *di san ge* 第三个 (the third one)---*san* 三 (three)! Or you can read the whole sentence in Chinese by simply following the *Pinyin* guide on the right and listening to the audio resources.
Remember: Practice makes perfect!

PLAYING INTERACTIVE GAMES:
You can play games. Cut out the game cards on page 33 and 35.
Here are two ways to play!

1. Matching game! Pick a card. Find the corresponding page in the book, and say the number in Chinese.
For example: *Instructor:* look, what card I just picked!
Child: three! *Instructor: san* 三, Let's find which page *san* is on!
Child: (looking in the book) I found *san* 三, *san* 三!
Instructor: (pointing to the fish on the page) Let's count, *yi* 一 *er* 二, *san* 三 (one, two, three)

2. Math game! Create a math equation using the cards. Pick two number cards, a plus or minus sign, and an equal sign. Solve the equation. Then find the corresponding number card. Lastly, find the page in the book with that number. Whoever finds the nunber first and shouts it out in Chinese wins!

LEARNING MORE VOCABULARY:
You can learn more through the following additional resources!
1. Grammar explanations and useful words/phrases on page 5
2. List of numbers 11 to 100 on page 32

LISTENING TO THE AUDIO RESOURCE:
Please visit www.yuechenart.com for the audio and video resources including: Pinyin guide, vocabulary page and the story read aloud in Chinese. You may contact *meimeistory@yuechenart.com* with questions, comments, and suggestions!

USING THE PINYIN GUIDE:
In this book, you will see English, Pinyin and Chinese characters. *Pinyin*, or *Hanyu Pinyin* (as it is known formally) is the official system to transcribe Chinese characters into Latin script in the People's Republic of China, Taiwan and Singapore. Some *Pinyin* sounds are similar to English sounds, and others are quite different.
The table below will help you learn the pronunciations. The *Pinyin* system also uses diacritics to mark the four tones of Mandarin. The first tone (Flat or High Level Tone) '¯', the second tone (Rising or High-Rising Tone) '´', the third tone (Falling-Rising or Low Tone) 'ˇ' and the fourth tone (Falling or High-Falling Tone) '`'. Briefly, the tone mark should always be placed above vowels ---a o e i u ù. You can also use the audio resources listed on the left to help you learn to pronounce syllables, and vowels with the four tones in the *Pinyin* system.

Pinyin	English	*Pinyin*	English
b	s**p**it	ou	**s**o
p	**p**ay	an	**b**an
m	**m**ay	en	tak**en**
f	**f**air	ang	s**ong**
d	s**t**op	eng	**Kung** fu
t	**t**ake	ia	**ya**rd
n	**l**ean	ie	**ye**t
l	**l**ay	in	**inn**
g	s**k**ill	ian	**yen**
k	o**k**ay	ing	d**ing**
h	**h**old	u	**too**
j	**j**eep	ü	*French 'lune'*
q	**chee**tah	o,ou	**o**
x	**she**	uai	**why**
z	rea**ds**	ui	**we**
c	**hats**	uan	**won**
s	**s**ay	un	**win**
i	**it**	ong	**own**
a	**father**	zh	**j**unk
e	**foot**	ch	**ch**urch
ai	**eye**	sh	**sh**irt
ei	h**ey**	r	**r**ay
ao	c**ow**	w	**w**ay
		y	**y**es

USEFUL WORDS & PHRASES

dinner	wǎn cān 晚 餐
mom	mā ma 妈 妈
to wait	děng 等
...is waiting for...	zài děng 在 等
and	hé 和
she/her	tā/tā 她／她
siblings	xiōng dì jiě mèi 兄 弟 姐 妹
come back	huí lái 回 来
with	hé 和
to play	wán / wán er 玩 ／ 玩儿
...is playing...	zài wán / zài wán er 在 玩 ／ 在 玩 儿
hide and seek	zhuō mí cáng 捉 迷 藏
to say	shuō 说

to help	bāng/bāng máng 帮 ／ 帮 忙
to find	zhǎo 找
they/them	tā men/tā men 他 们／他 们
I/me	wǒ/wǒ 我 ／我
we/us	wǒ men 我 们
together	yì qǐ 一 起
to look for...	zhǎo yì zhǎo 找 一 找
as long as...	zhǐ yào 只 要
You (Singular)	nǐ 你
You (plural)	nǐ men 你 们
to help one another	hù xiāng bāng zhù 互 相 帮 助
can	néng 能

where is '2'? (page 11,13,15,17,19,21,23,25,27)

In Chinese, the interrogative pronoun stays at the end of the sentence.

The literal translation in Chinese is: *2 is at where?* èr zài nǎ er
二在哪儿?

Meimei is still playing hide-and-seek with her siblings. (page 7)

The literal translation in Chinese is: *Meimei with her siblings is still playing hide-and seek.*
Mei mei hé tā de xiōng dì jiě mèi zài wán er zhuō mí cáng
美 美 和 她 的 兄 弟 姐 妹 在 玩 儿 捉 迷 藏。

Can you help me find them? (page 8)

can: néng 能 *I* **can** *fly* *I* **néng** *fly*.

Can...? : néng...ma 能...吗? **Can** *you fly?* *you* **néng** *fly* **ma?**

The literal translation in Chinese is: *you* **néng** *help me find them* **ma?**
nǐ néng bāng wǒ zhǎo dào tā men ma
你 能 帮 我 找 到 他 们 吗?

Let's look for it together... (page 11,13,15,17,19,21,23,25,27)

The literal translation in Chinese is: *let us together look for...*
ràng wǒ men yì qǐ zhǎo yì zhǎo
让 我 们 一 起 找 一 找......

It's **dinner** time!
wǎn cān shí jiān dào le
晚 餐 时 间 到 了!

Meimei's **mom** **is waiting for** Meimei **and** her **siblings** to **come back** for dinner.
měi měi de **mā ma zài děng** měi měi **hé** tā de **xiōng dì jiě mèi** **huí lái** chī wǎn cān
美 美 的 妈 妈 在 等 美 美 和 她 的 兄 弟 姐 妹 回 来 吃 晚 餐。

Meimei **is** still **playing hide-and-seek** with her siblings.
měi měi hé tā de xiōng dì jiě mèi hái **zài wán** **zhuō mí cáng**
美 美 和 她 的 兄 弟 姐 妹 还 在 玩 捉 迷 藏。

Note: please see further grammar explanations in the "useful words and phrases" section located on page 5.

Mom says: Can you **help me** find them?
mā ma shuō: nǐ néng **bāng wǒ** zhǎo dào tā men ma
妈 妈 说: 你 能 帮 我 找 到 他 们 吗?

Note: please see further grammar explanations in the "useful words and phrases" section located on page 5.

Meimei says: Okay! No problem!
měi měi shuō hǎo méi wèn tí
美 美 说： 好！ 没 问 题！

Aha!   I found **the first one** ---- **ONE!**
hā ha wǒ zhǎo dào le **dì yī gè   yī**
哈 哈！ 我 找   到 了 第 一 个 ---- 一！

But where is **the second one**? Where is '**two**'?
dàn shì **dì èr gè** zài nǎ er **èr** zài nǎ er
但是， 第二个在 哪儿? '二' 在 哪儿?

Uhm...Let's look for it together...
en ràng wǒ men yì qǐ zhǎo yì zhǎo
嗯......让 我 们 一 起 找 一 找......

Note: please see further grammar explanations in the "useful words and phrases" section located on page 5.

Aha! We found **the second one** ---- **TWO** !
hā ha wǒ men zhǎo dào le **dì èr gè**   **èr**
哈哈! 我 们 找   到 了 第二个 ---- 二!

But   where is **the third one**?   where is '**three**'?
dàn shì   **dì sān gè** zài nǎ er   **sān** zài nǎ er
但是， 第 三 个 在 哪儿?   '三' 在 哪儿?

Uhm...Let's look for it together...
en   ràng wǒ men yì qǐ zhǎo yì zhǎo
嗯......让 我 们 一 起 找 一 找......

13

Note: please see further grammar explanations in the "useful words and phrases" section located on page 5.

Aha! We found **the third one** ---- **THREE**!
hā ha wǒ men zhǎo dào le **dì sān gè**   **sān**
哈哈！我 们 找 到 了 第三个 ---- 三！

14

But   where is **the fourth one**? Where is '**four**'?
dàn shì **dì sì gè** zài nǎ er   **sì** zài nǎ er
但是，第四个 在哪儿?   '四' 在哪 儿?

Uhm...Let's look for it together...
en   ràng wǒ men yì qǐ zhǎo yì zhǎo
嗯......让 我 们一起找一找......

Note: please see further grammar explanations in the "useful words and phrases" section located on page 5.

Aha! We found **the fourth one** ---- **FOUR!**
hā ha   wǒ men zhǎo dào le **dì sì gè   sì**
哈哈！ 我 们 找 到 了 第四个 ---- 四！

But   where is **the fifth one**?   Where is '**five**'?
dàn shì   **dì wǔ gè** zài nǎ er   **wǔ** zài nǎ er
但 是, 第五个 在 哪 儿?   '五' 在 哪 儿?

Uhm...Let's look for it together...
en   ràng wǒ men yì qǐ zhǎo yì zhǎo
嗯......让 我 们 一 起 找 一 找......

17

Note: please see further grammar explanations in the "useful words and phrases" section located on page 5.

Aha! We found **the fifth one** ---- **FIVE**!

hā ha wǒ men zhǎo dào le **dì wǔ gè wǔ**

哈哈！我们找到了第五个----五！

But where is **the sixth one**? Where is '**six**'?
dàn shì **dì liù gè** zài nǎ er **liù** zài nǎ er
但是，第六个在哪儿？ '六'在哪儿？

Uhm...Let's look for it together...
en ràng wǒ men yì qǐ zhǎo yì zhǎo
嗯......让 我 们 一 起 找 一 找......

Aha!   We found **the sixth one** ---- **SIX**!
hā ha wǒ men zhǎo dào le **dì liù gè   liù**
哈哈！ 我 们 找 到 了 第六个 ---- 六！

But   where is **the seventh one**? Where is '**seven**'?
dàn shì **dì qī gè** zài nǎ er   **qī** zài nǎ er
但是，第七个在哪儿？   '七'在 哪儿？

Uhm...Let's look for it together...
en   ràng wǒ men yì qǐ zhǎo yì zhǎo
嗯......让 我 们 一 起 找 一 找......

Note: please see further grammar explanations in the "useful words and phrases" section located on page 5.

Aha! We found **the seventh one** ----SEVEN!

hā ha   wǒ men zhǎo dào le **dì qī gè**   **qī**

哈哈! 我 们 找 到 了第七个----七!

But   where is **the eighth one**?   Where is '**eight**'?
dàn shì   **dì bā gè** zài nǎ er   **bā**   zài nǎ er
但是，**第八个** 在哪儿?   '**八**' 在哪儿?

Uhm...Let's look for it together...
en   ràng wǒ men yì qǐ zhǎo yì zhǎo
嗯......让 我 们 一 起 找 一 找......

23

please see further grammar explanations in the "useful words and phrases" section located on page 5.

Aha!   We found **the eighth one** ---- **EIGHT!**
hā ha   wǒ men zhǎo dào le **dì bā gè**   **bā**
哈哈！ 我 们 找 到 了 第八个 ---- 八！

But   where is **the ninth one**?   Where is '**nine**'?
dàn shì   **dì jiǔ gè** zài nǎ er   **jiǔ**   zài nǎ er
但是，第九个在哪儿?   '九'在哪儿?

Uhm...Let's look for it together...
en   ràng wǒ men yì qǐ zhǎo yì zhǎo
嗯......让 我 们 一 起 找 一 找......

Note: please see further grammar explanations in the "useful words and phrases" section located on page 5.

Aha! We found **the ninth one** ---- **NINE**!
hā ha wǒ men zhǎo dào le **dì jiǔ gè   jiǔ**
哈哈! 我 们 找 到 了 第九个 ---- 九!

But   where is **the tenth one**?   Where is '**ten**'?
dàn shì **dì shí gè** zài nǎ er   **shí**, zài nǎ er
但是， 第十个 在 哪 儿?   '十' 在 哪 儿?

Uhm...Let's look for it together...
en   ràng wǒ men yì qǐ zhǎo yì zhǎo
嗯......让 我 们 一 起 找 一 找......

27

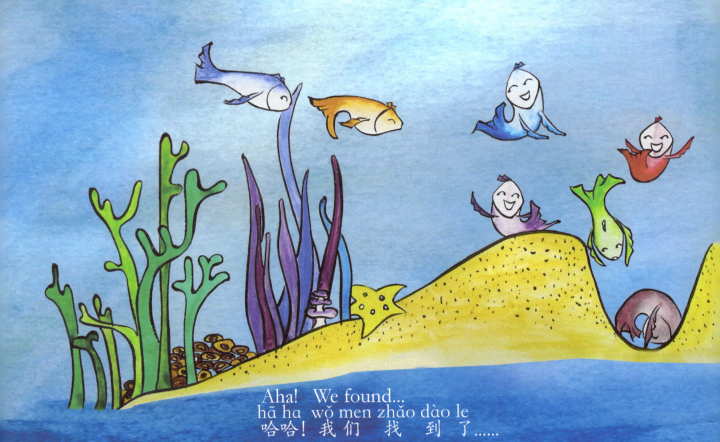

Aha! We found...
hā ha wǒ men zhǎo dào le
哈哈！我们　找　到　了......

... the tenth one ---- TEN!
dì shí gè   shí
......第 十 个 ---- 十!

See, as long as you **help one another**, you **can** do it!

kàn   zhǐ yào nǐ men **hù xiāng bāng zhù**   nǐ men jiù **néng** xíng

看，只 要 你 们 互 相 帮 助，你 们 就 能 行！

Note: please see further grammar explanations in the "useful words and phrases" section located on page 5.

Let's count,
ràng wǒ men shǔ yì shǔ
让 我 们 数 一 数,

one, two, three, four, five, six, seven, eight, nine, ten!
yī èr sān sì wǔ liù qī bā jiǔ shí
一, 二, 三, 四, 五, 六, 七, 八, 九, 十!

Vocabulary

shí 十	10	sān shí jiǔ 三十九	39
shí yī 十一	11	sì shí 四十	40
shí èr 十二	12	sì shí yī 四十一	41
shí sān 十三	13	sì shí èr 四十二	42
shí sì 十四	14	·	
shí wǔ 十五	15	sì shí jiǔ 四十九	49
shí liù 十六	16	wǔ shí 五十	50
shí qī 十七	17	wǔ shí yī 五十一	51
shí bā 十八	18	wǔ shí èr 五十二	52
shí jiǔ 十九	19	·	
èr shí 二十	20	wǔ shí jiǔ 五十九	59
èr shí yī 二十一	21	liù shí 六十	60
èr shí èr 二十二	22	liù shí yī 六十一	61
·		liù shí èr 六十二	62
èr shí jiǔ 二十九	29	·	
sān shí 三十	30	liù shí jiǔ 六十九	69
sān shí yī 三十一	31		
sān shí èr 三十二	32		

qī shí 七十	70
qī shí yī 七十一	71
qī shí èr 七十二	72
·	
qī shí jiǔ 七十九	79
bā shí 八十	80
bā shí yī 八十一	81
bā shí èr 八十二	82
·	
bā shí jiǔ 八十九	89
jiǔ shí 九十	90
jiǔ shí yī 九十一	91
jiǔ shí èr 九十二	92
·	
jiǔ shí jiǔ 九十九	99
yì bǎi 一百	100

Game card 1

yī
一

1

èr
二

2

sān
三

3

sì
四

4

wǔ
五

5

liù
六

6

Game card 2

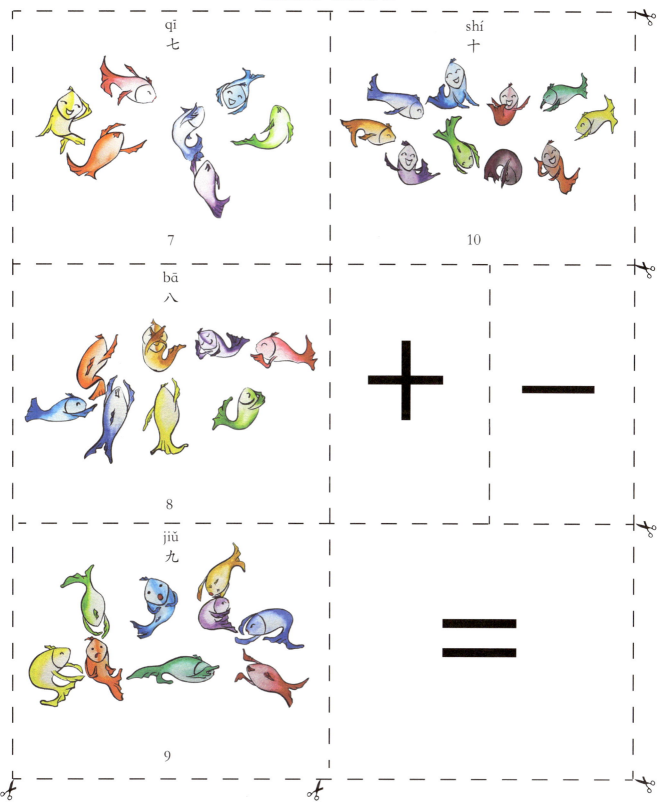

qī
七

7

shí
十

10

bā
八

8

$+$ $-$

jiǔ
九

9

$=$

CPSIA information can be obtained
at www.ICGtesting.com
Printed in the USA
LVHW07n1721260718
585039LV00012B/123/P